Be the Boss of your STRESS
Self-Care for Kids

Timothy Culbert, M.D., and Rebecca Kajander, C.P.N.P., M.P.H.

"The most useful and wise book series for children that I have ever seen."
—Lonnie Zeltzer, M.D.
Director of Pediatric Pain Program, UCLA Mattel Children's Hospital

"Practical, enjoyable ways to enhance [children's] self-care abilities. Has positive implications for an entire lifetime."
—Karen Olness, M.D.
Professor of Pediatrics and Director Emeritus, Developmental/Behavioral Pediatrics Department at Rainbow Babies and Children's Hospital, Cleveland, Ohio

"Clear, practical . . . excellent series on self-care for kids. I recommend it highly."
—Andrew Weil, M.D.
Director, Program in Integrative Medicine, University of Arizona, and author of *8 Weeks to Optimum Health*

free spirit
PUBLiSHiNG®

Helping kids
help themselves™
since 1983

Be the
BOSS
of your
BODY™

Library of Congress Cataloging-in-Publication Data
Culbert, Timothy.
  Be the boss of your stress : self-care for kids / Timothy Culbert and Rebecca Kajander.
      p. cm.—(Be the boss of your body series)
    ISBN-13: 978-1-57542-256-5
    ISBN-10: 1-57542-256-5
  1. Stress management—Juvenile literature. 2. Stress management for children—Juvenile literature.
I. Kajander, Rebecca. II. Title.
  RA785.C83 2007
  616.9'80083—dc22
                                                                        2006102856

The concepts, ideas, procedures, and suggestions contained in this book are not intended as substitutes for professional healthcare.

The people depicted on the cover and throughout this book are models and used for illustrative purposes only.

Edited by Eric Braun and Douglas J. Fehlen
Illustrated by Tuko Fujisaki
Cover and interior design by Calico

10 9 8 7 6 5 4 3 2 1
Made in China

Free Spirit Publishing Inc.
217 Fifth Avenue North, Suite 200
Minneapolis, MN 55401-1299
(612) 338-2068
help4kids@freespirit.com
www.freespirit.com

Free Spirit Publishing is a member of the Green Press Initiative, and we're committed to printing our books on recycled paper containing a minimum of 30% post-consumer waste (PCW). For every ton of books printed on 30% PCW recycled paper, we save 5.1 trees, 2,100 gallons of water, 114 gallons of oil, 18 pounds of air pollution, 1,230 kilowatt hours of energy, and .9 cubic yards of landfill space. At Free Spirit it's our goal to nurture not only young people, but nature too!

Dedication

To Heidi, Samuel, and Hannah, with all my love, and to William and Joanne Culbert, with special thanks for their love and support. —T.C.

To Tim, my friend and colleague for his endless support, encouragement, and good humor. —R.K.

Acknowledgments

Our continuing respect and gratitude to the pioneers of pediatric mind-body-spirit skills: Drs. Karen Olness, Daniel Kohen, Judson Reaney, Candace Erickson, Lonnie Zeltzer, and Leora Kuttner. Thank you to Dr. Carolyn Torkelson for reading and commenting on the book. We'd also like to extend our gratitude to Judy Galbraith for supporting this important project, as well as Eric Braun and the entire fun-loving team at Free Spirit Publishing for their ability to turn our ideas into reality. Finally, thanks to all the wonderful and talented children and families with whom we have been privileged to collaborate and from whom we have learned so much.

Contents

Important Note (Don't Skip This!)

In this book you'll learn ways to take charge of your health. But even though you're the one taking charge, it's still a good idea to get parents or other family adults involved, too. Show them this book, including the "Note to Grown-Ups" on page 54. Let them know how you're feeling and how it's going. You also can ask them to help you practice the skills you're learning, make changes to your lifestyle, and celebrate your successes!

Super Important Part: This book doesn't replace the need to use healthcare professionals, like doctors and nurses. It's true that you'll be happier and healthier if you are the boss of your body and can take care of most of your stress on your own, but sometimes you need help. Be sure to tell your mom, dad, or other adult when you're not feeling well— they can help you decide if you should see a doctor. You can use the list on the next page to help you decide.

See a doctor if:

- stress feels worse instead of better after a few days
- stress causes you to have severe aches and pains or makes it hard for you to sleep
- your stress doesn't go away no matter what you do
- you get symptoms of illness like a fever and vomiting
- you are missing a lot of school
- you feel very sad or hopeless
- you worry that nothing is ever going to make you feel better

If you're not sure whether you should see a healthcare professional, go ahead and do it. It's better to be safe about your health than to wonder if things will get better. When you do see professionals, tell them you want to use the **self-care** approaches in this book. They will be happy to know you want to help yourself!

Self-care means just what it sounds like: things you can do your**self** to take **care** of yourself.

Your Body Is Amazing!

Everybody feels lousy from time to time. They get sick or have aches and pains, or they have trouble sleeping. Sometimes they get stressed out or just plain-old down in the dumps. Kids who feel bad sometimes believe only grown-ups—like doctors, nurses, or parents—can help them feel better. Some people may think only pills, shots, or surgery can help.

Those things *are* important at times. But wouldn't it be nice if you could make your*self* feel better—without a trip to the doctor or a bunch of medicine? What if you could do it just by taking care of yourself and believing that you will get better?

Your **body, mind,** and **spirit**—working together— have amazing abilities to heal you. Your body can take care of itself by healing wounds, killing germs, and fighting infections. It's like you have a hospital inside you that knows how to keep you healthy. Not only that, but you can also control how your body feels—even when you feel stressed.

Your body, mind, and spirit are the three main parts of your self. Turn to pages 6–7 to learn more.

3

You Can Be the Boss of Your Body!

It's true. Being the boss of your body means knowing that your body, mind, and spirit are connected and work together. It also means knowing how to use those connections to make yourself feel better and stay healthy. It's a way for you to be actively involved in your own health and wellness.

How Will This Book Help Me?

Practicing the skills and activities in this book can help you:

✓ feel less stress

✓ deal with stress in healthy ways

✓ make fewer visits to the doctor's office, emergency room, or hospital

✓ take less medicine

✓ feel better for school, sports, hobbies, and other activities

✓ have more fun with friends and family

Be the Boss of Your Stress

Part of being the boss of your body is being the boss over stress—whether it's stress about school, friends, or stuff happening at home. This book is filled with ideas, activities, and skills you can use to feel less stressed and more in charge of your health. You can use what you learn in this book for the rest of your life.

You can do most of the activities and skills with nothing more than a positive attitude and practicing every day. But there are tools, like stress balls and pinwheels, that can help you do the activities better and keep track of your progress. If you have the "Be the Boss of Your Body Kit," you already have those tools. If you don't have the kit, don't worry! You can do most of the skills and activities without anything extra, and you may be able to find some tools around your home.

We wrote this book to help you be the boss of your body, and we'd like to hear how it goes for you. You can email us at help4kids@freespirit.com or send us a letter at:

Free Spirit Publishing, 217 Fifth Avenue North, Suite 200
Minneapolis, MN 55401-1299

When you see the abbreviation B³ in this book, don't be confused—it's not a vitamin, an algebra problem, or a bingo square! B³ is our shortcut way of saying "Be the Boss of Your Body."

Let's get started!

What It Means to Be the Boss of Your Body

Being the boss of your body does **not** mean being **bossy** to other people!

Most kids think they are healthy if they brush their teeth, don't eat too much candy, and are not sick. And it's true, those are signs of good health, but being healthy is a lot more than just having a physical body that is fit and well. It's also having a healthy, positive mind and spirit. Your body, mind, and spirit are connected and work together. Being the boss of your body means taking charge of all three to help yourself deal with common problems and feel your best.

What Is Your Body?

You know what your body is. It's the physical part of yourself—all of your bones, muscles, organs, and everything else about you that takes up space in the world. You know your own body better than anyone else. You know your strengths and weaknesses, and you know how you feel when you are healthy or sick.

When you eat well, exercise, get enough rest, and manage stress, your body runs well and fights off illnesses. You stay healthy. The reverse also is true—if you don't take care of your body, it has a harder time staying healthy.

What Is Your Mind?

Your mind is the part of you that thinks, understands, remembers, imagines, and feels emotions. When you picture an image in your head or try to figure out a problem, you're using your mind. You're also using your mind when you think thoughts, or "talk" to yourself in your head. That's called **self-talk,** and having positive self-talk is a great way to keep your mind healthy, fit, and happy.

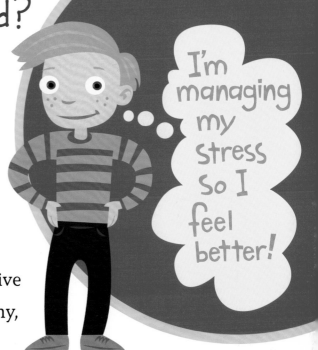

I'm managing my stress so I feel better!

What Is Your Spirit?

"Spirit" can mean a lot of different things. In this book we are not talking about ghosts, and we're not talking about school spirit. We're talking about something inside you that gives you feelings of hope, comfort, and peace. Your spirit connects you to things outside yourself and gives life meaning. For many people, a healthy spirit has to do with a belief in God or a higher power. A healthy spirit can also come from a feeling of connection with music, art, or nature. Spiritual health is a feeling you have inside of being content or peaceful.

How Balance Can Help

When your body, mind, and spirit are all healthy and positive, they help each other *stay* healthy and positive. When this happens, we say the three are "balanced." That means they are fit and strong—each in their own way but also together—to make a whole, healthy, fabulous you!

What does it feel like to be balanced?

YOUR MIND

* You have positive thoughts and emotions.

* You feel confident, loved, grateful, proud, and safe.

* You feel organized and able to focus attention.

YOUR BODY

* You have warm fingers and toes.

* Your breathing and heartbeat are regular.

* The palms of your hands are dry.

* Your muscles are relaxed.

YOUR SPIRIT

* You notice and appreciate beauty.

* You feel connected to and loved by others.

* You have a sense of peacefulness.

* You enjoy nature.

* You may feel some identification with God or a higher power.

* You may engage in regular practice of meditation or prayer.

The Power of the Positive

If you're stressed out, the best way to get back to feeling your best is to do things that will help your body, mind, *and* spirit. People who

+ eat well and get enough exercise and sleep
+ think positively and believe they can help themselves
+ feel hopeful, peaceful, and supported by loved ones

have an easier time handling stress. They get sick less often and they recover quicker from sickness and injury.

Who's the Boss?

You are the boss of your body. You can control your heart rate, breathing, hand temperature, and muscle tension—and other things that help you relax and feel better—just by thinking about them.

You are the boss of your mind. You can create positive and calming thoughts and control negative emotions and worried thoughts. All thoughts and feelings affect how your body feels.

You are the boss of your spirit. You can take a walk in a favorite place; pray or meditate; or sing, play, or listen to music, all of which can help your body feel good.

You are the boss of your life. People who do self-care skills and activities, and who are balanced in all three areas, usually live longer and healthier lives.

To successfully be the boss of all these things, it's important that **you** make the choice to do it. Learn self-care skills and activities for yourself, not for your mom or dad or a doctor or nurse, because your own motivation is what makes you successful. That doesn't mean you don't need coaching, love, support, and advice from family, friends, healthcare providers, or teachers. It just means you have to do this for you.

I'm Stressed Out!

You've probably heard people talk a lot about being stressed. Parents might have things they're worried about at work or concerns about money. But stress doesn't affect only adults—it bothers kids, too. You've probably felt stressed yourself—maybe when you had too much homework an argument with a friend.

"I feel like my brain is on overload!"

Stress is related to the "fight-or-flight response." When people are surprised or worried, the body's first reaction is often DANGER!!! The fight-or-flight response provides a boost of energy that helps to either face danger or get away from it. This reaction has helped human beings survive for millions of years.

What Is Stress?

Stress is your body's reaction to things that worry you or make you feel unsure. When you are upset or anxious about something, your body produces adrenaline and other energy-boosting chemicals. Here's what happens:

- Your heartbeat and breathing speed up.
- More blood goes pumping to your heart and big muscles.
- Muscles become tense and get ready to move.
- Your hands get sweaty.
- Digestion slows down.
- Your mouth gets dry.
- You need to use the bathroom more than usual.
- It becomes harder for you to think clearly.
- You feel like your body is all tied up in knots.

These are all signs of stress. Stress can actually come in handy over short periods of time. Think of a big test you had at school. Worrying about it probably made you study hard so that you could do your best. This kind of short-term stress is healthy and can help you.

How Stress Can Hurt You

When stress stays around too long, you might feel anxious or afraid—even when there's no real reason to be worried. Stress that lasts for a long time can put your body, mind, and spirit out of balance. You might:

- get headaches, stomachaches, or other body pains
- become sick more easily
- feel angry, sad, or depressed
- sleep much more or less than you did before
- eat much more or less than you did before
- cry more often than usual
- skip school or quit trying to do your work
- tease, argue, or fight with others

If any of these things are happening to you, it's important to speak with an adult you trust right away.

Things That Can Stress Out Kids

If you feel stressed out at times, you're not alone. Most kids say they sometimes worry a lot or feel too busy. Here are some things they say stress them out:

* too much homework

* timed tests

* parents' fighting

* missing school

* problems with friends

* too many things to do

* family financial problems

* parents pressuring them to do things

* getting in trouble when it's not their fault

* moving to a new community and school

* being sick a lot or for a long time

* negative thoughts about themselves

* grades

* parents' separation or divorce

* weather (like floods or hurricanes)

* environmental problems

* violence on television

* being teased or bullied

anything and everything!

What Can You Do?

You might not be able to prevent stressful events but you can control your reaction to them. The B³ skills you're learning can help you handle stress better. And there are many other positive (and fun) ways to be the boss of your stress.

Six Quick Tips to Sack Stress

1. Talk to someone you love and trust. When you're really worried about a problem, it can feel like you need to deal with it on your own. But family members and friends are there to love and support you. Just talking about something that is bothering you can make you feel a lot better. Plus, this person might have ideas for solving a problem.

Whew! It feels good to get that off my chest!

2. Stay positive. When you feel bad about something, it can be hard to stop thinking about it and thinking about it and. . . . Okay, you get the idea. Instead, think positively. When you tell yourself that you can overcome mistakes and bad feelings, you're better able to.

3. Have a laugh! Many experts believe that laughter is great medicine against stress. When you're feeling twisted up in knots, find some humor in the comics section of the newspaper. Read a funny book or watch a hilarious movie. Whatever it is that makes you chuckle, laughing it up can help your stress feel lighter.

4. Stay active and have fun. Whether it's hanging out with friends, biking around the neighborhood, or reading the latest book in your favorite series, find cool things you like to do. You might pick up a fun hobby that makes you feel happy and calm.

5. Take care of yourself. Regular meals, sleep, and exercise are all important toward reducing stress. Also avoid too much caffeine, which can make you feel edgy and tense. (Find more info on these everyday ways to handle stress on pages 48–52.)

6. Stick with your daily routines. Stress can make you want to climb under your bed and never come out. But there's no surer way to let stress get the best of you than to stop doing the things you usually do. Problems at school or with friends won't be solved if you avoid them. Hiding out from tough situations can even make them seem worse.

Checkup For Your Body, Mind, and Spirit

Most people aren't aware of all the ways stress affects them—that's why it's important to go through a **whole-self checkup.** Once you understand how stress affects your body, mind, and spirit, you can begin to change things for the better using the B³ skills.

Start by thinking about your stress. Maybe you're worried about certain things—like your grades at school, how you'll play in the big game, or the health of a loved one. Or you might feel stressed all the time about lots of different things. However you feel, think about how stress affects your life. Are there things you usually enjoy but that aren't very fun right now? Look at the list on page 19 and put a checkmark next to all the things that are harder or just less fun for you because of stress. At the bottom of the list, add any other things that stress interferes with. Make more lines if you need to.

Stress interferes with these things in my ...

- ☐ playing or working on the computer
- ☐ doing fun things with family
- ☐ going to a place of worship
- ☐ concentrating on homework
- ☐ physical activities or sports
- ☐ playing with friends
- ☐ enjoying art or music
- ☐ being out in nature
- ☐ enjoying hobbies
- ☐ going to school
- ☐ watching TV
- ☐ sleeping
- ☐ eating
- ☐ other_____
- ☐ other_____
- ☐ other_____

Imagine how great it will be when you can do these things with less stress getting in the way!

...ɔoes Your Stress Feel Like?

...at the pictures on page 21. Imagine that body is your body, and place an **X** on the spots where stress affects you. These might be places where you feel tension, aches, or pains. If you'd like, you can make a small **x** on spots where you feel a little stress, and a big **X** where stress affects you a lot. Then, answer the questions on the lines below.

Write down as many words as you can think of that describe how stress makes you feel (like edgy, panicky, nervous, I'm-tied-in-knots, it-stinks-I-hate-it, freaked out, or others):

_____

_____

_____

What other feelings or problems is your stress causing? Are you tired or dizzy? Do you feel like throwing up? Do you have diarrhea or trouble sleeping? Are you more or less hungry than usual? Do you feel sad, scared, angry, or bored? This is the place to write down **anything** you think has changed because of the stress you feel.

_____

_____

_____

_____

Front

Back

21

Brain/Body Scan

Ask a parent, brother or sister, or friend to help you with this activity, which can help you be more aware of how you're feeling. Lie down or sit in a comfortable chair and have your helper read the following exercise to you. The person should read in a calm, steady voice, pausing between sentences to give you time to think about them. Become more and more aware of your body as you go. It should take three to five minutes to do.

Think about how your body feels in lots of different ways. Starting with your head and moving slowly down your body to your toes, notice your muscles: Are they tight or loose? Sore or comfortable? Heavy or light feeling? Think about your skin: Is it dry or moist? Warm or cool? Smooth or rough? Notice how your clothing feels against your skin: Tight, loose, smooth, rough, scratchy? Notice the chair you're sitting in or floor or bed you're laying on, and become aware of how it feels against your body: Where do you feel the most pressure? Is it soft or hard? Next, notice your heart beating. Notice your breathing. Notice the thoughts that pass through your mind, but try not to judge or react to them—just let them pass through. Notice light and shadows in the room. Notice smells and sounds, or silence.

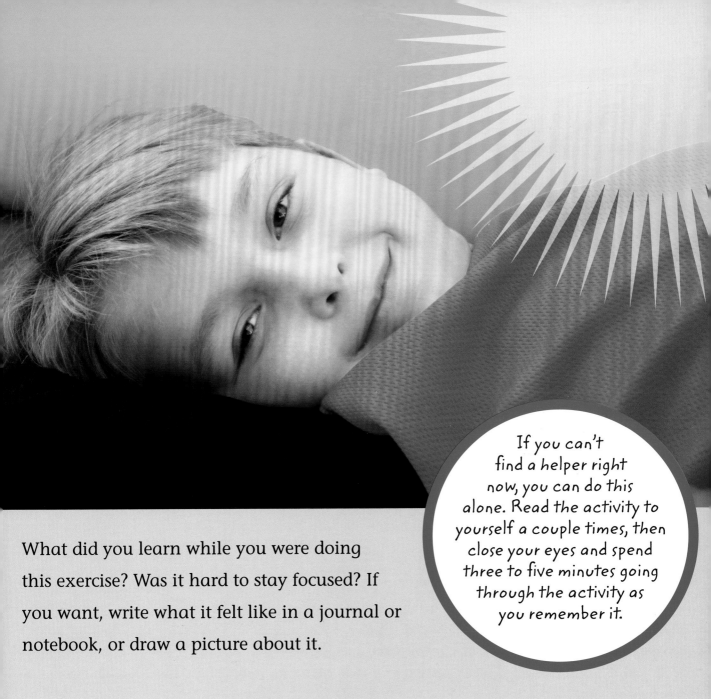

What did you learn while you were doing this exercise? Was it hard to stay focused? If you want, write what it felt like in a journal or notebook, or draw a picture about it.

If you can't find a helper right now, you can do this alone. Read the activity to yourself a couple times, then close your eyes and spend three to five minutes going through the activity as you remember it.

Rate Your Body, Mind, and Spirit

It's time to really think about how your body, mind, and spirit are doing. You can do that by looking at the three measuring sticks on the next page: the **Body-O-Meter,** the **Mind-O-Meter,** and the **Spirit-O-Meter.** For each one, read the description on both ends of the meter and give yourself a rating from 1 to 10. If you want to, write your score in your journal.

Body~O~Meter

You feel energetic, relaxed, pain free, comfortable, or just right.

10
9
8
7
6
5
4
3
2
1
0

You feel tense, tired, painful, uncomfortable, or just not right.

Mind~O~Meter

You have mostly positive, helpful thoughts and feelings, like happiness, pride, and confidence.

10
9
8
7
6
5
4
3
2
1
0

You have mostly negative or unhelpful thoughts and feelings, like anger, sadness, and boredom.

Spirit~O~Meter

You feel connected to others, nature, or a higher power such as God.

10
9
8
7
6
5
4
3
2
1
0

You feel lonely, out of touch, like life doesn't have meaning.

How Would You **Like** to Feel?

Now that you know how you feel, think about how you would *like* to feel. Of course you would like to feel better—but what does that mean, exactly? It's time to set some specific goals for yourself.

To start, imagine a stress-free day. Think about this in very specific ways, with lots of details. How would this day be different from today? What would you do that you can't do now? How do you want to feel? Think about some of the things you do every day, like eating, sleeping, going to school, and playing with friends. How will these things be different on your stress-free day? Will they be easier or more fun? Why?

Write down your ideas:

_____

_____

_____

_____

_____

Now write down three specific, important things you will do when you feel less stressed:

1. _____

_____

_____

2. _____

_____

_____

3. _____

_____

_____

_____

Take Control of Stress

It's time to learn the B³ skills and start practicing them! It's best to practice all of the skills several times so you can figure out which ones you like using and which work best to help you feel less stress.

If you can, try the skills for the first few times when you are not feeling anxious—it's easier to get the hang of them that way. But if you're feeling stressed right now, that's okay. Jump right in!

Practice the skills two or three times a day until you are comfortable with them. The B³ skills are just like other things you have learned and gotten good at, like writing your name or riding a bike. The more you practice, the better you get at it and the easier it is. Once you've got the B³ skills down, they'll be there to help you forever, and you can use them anywhere you are.

Get Comfy!

You'll have better luck with these skills if you make yourself as comfortable as possible before you begin:

● Wear clothes that are loose and comfortable.

● If you like music, put on music that is quiet and familiar. Otherwise, make sure it's quiet, so there are no distractions.

● Turn the lights low or off.

● Make sure you have a chair, pillows, blankets—whatever you like to keep yourself comfortable.

● Give yourself some privacy by choosing a place where nobody will bug you.

What About Things I'm Already Doing?

If you are already taking medicine, doing physical therapy, seeing a doctor or psychologist, or getting other helpful treatments, keep doing those things. Some kids who use β^3 skills can reduce the amount of medicine or other treatments they need, but it's important to be careful about making changes. Talk with your doctor, therapist, or whoever is helping you to make sure you are getting all the treatment you need.

Skill 1: Belly Breathing

You already know you can control your breathing—you can hold your breath, and you can breathe fast or slow. Belly Breathing is a way of controlling your breathing to help you feel more relaxed.

When to Use It: Use Belly Breathing regularly to keep your body, mind, and spirit healthy and balanced and to feel less stress. You might use Belly Breathing when something is starting to stress you out and you feel it could get worse.

Why It Can Help: Belly Breathing relaxes your muscles, calms your nerves, and helps release chemicals (called *endorphins*) in your body that reduce pain.

What You Need: You need a comfortable place to sit or lie down.

How to Do It:

1. Imagine you have a balloon in your belly.

2. Put your hand on top of your belly.

3. Breathe in slowly through your nose, counting to three and feeling the balloon fill with air.

4. Breathe out slowly through your mouth, counting to five and feeling the balloon get flat. Imagine that the pain goes out of your body as you breathe out.

5. Notice how your muscles relax as you breathe out. Imagine a picture of your muscles relaxing.

Everyone breathes at a different rate, but most kids breathe about 20,000 times every 24 hours.

One way to make **Belly Breathing** more fun—and to help you see the results—is to use items such as a pinwheel, bubbles and bubble wand, or even a harmonica! While you are exhaling slowly you can do one of the following:

✷ Keep the pinwheel spinning for three to four seconds.

✷ Blow out through the straw part of the pinwheel (just take the top off) to help slow down your breathing.

✷ Blow long, slow streams of bubbles from the soapy wand.

✷ Sustain a note while blowing on the harmonica for three to four seconds.

Skill 2: Imagine That!

It might seem hard to believe, but changing what you're thinking about can completely change the way you feel.

When to Use It: Use Imagine That! regularly to keep your body, mind, and spirit healthy and balanced and to feel more relaxed. Imagine That! can also help you get rid of headaches and stomachaches that can result from stress.

Why It Can Help: Your mind is like a supercomputer that controls your body—and you can program your brain's "software." Creating pleasant, positive, healthy images in your mind can help you feel relaxed.

What You Need: You need a comfortable, quiet place.

How to Do It: Sit or lie down in your comfortable place. As a warm-up, do the first exercise on page 33, "Let your brain be a TV," to help you get the hang of using the power of your imagination. Then try each of the exercises that follow. As you do these, keep in mind that they work better the more involved your brain is, so give your brain plenty of details. Imagine lots of colors, shapes, and objects. Hear pleasant sounds, smell smells that please you, and notice what you can touch or what touches you. Make it all comforting and relaxing.

Let your brain be a TV. Imagine this: your brain is a TV and YOU are in charge of the remote control! Close your eyes and imagine that you turn on the TV and see your favorite food. What does it look like? Notice lots of details. Now change the channel and see your best friend, or a parent or brother or sister who makes you happy. Next, see your favorite character from a book, TV show, or movie. See? You can change the channel. That means you can change your thinking to help yourself feel less stressed.

Imagine fun. Imagine you are somewhere that is fun, safe, and pleasant for you. Picture yourself doing something you really enjoy, like playing a sport, reading a book, or playing with a dog or cat. Remember to imagine lots of details. As you do this, notice how your body feels. Is it relaxing? Is your stress melting away? Many positive images can help you feel less stress, so you may want to experiment with different ones until you find the pictures that help you the most.

Ride in a hot air balloon. Ride in a hot air balloon. Imagine you are sitting in the basket of a very colorful and comfortable hot air balloon. This hot air balloon has a special connection to your body, mind, and spirit, because your positive thoughts and feelings make the balloon fly. Breathe slowly, relax your muscles, and think of something that makes you feel happy and secure, such as your love for your family. Imagine your feelings of love filling the balloon with air. Feel the basket leave the ground as you begin to drift into the sky. Now, think of a day when you were very happy. As you remember lots of details from this day, see the balloon swell with the warm, good memories. Feel yourself rise higher and higher until you, too, are filled with warm good feelings, just like the balloon. Your hot air balloon soars high over any beautiful place you choose—it might be lovely, snow-capped mountains, a shimmering blue-green sea, or a lush, quiet forest. Spend as much time as you like on this amazing journey and when you are ready, gently land the balloon in a spot that you pick. As you come back to your usual state of awareness, notice the pleasant sensation of lightness in your body.

Use the jettison technique. "Jettison" means getting rid of something by throwing it away from you. Hold a stress ball, or something soft you can safely squeeze in one hand (like rolled-up socks, a beanbag, or a small pillow). Then think of all the stress and tension and sleep-stopping thoughts that have built up inside you. Start squeezing the ball or object in your hand and imagine all that sleep-stopping stuff is traveling from your brain, down your arm, into your hand, and being squeezed right out of your hand into the ball! Then gently toss the ball onto a chair or the floor. Notice how quickly and gently your sleep can find you now, and how easily you can slide into pleasant dreams.

If you have a biofeedback card (you can get one at most drug stores), use it to see how your body changes as you do these imagination exercises. Biofeedback cards measure the temperature of your finger or thumb, which tells you how much stress you're feeling. Colder fingers mean more stress (and more stress means it's harder to sleep). Before you start, check your finger temperature. Then practice one of the **Imagine That!** exercises on pages 32–35 for three to five minutes and check your finger temperature again. Did it go up, go down, or stay the same? For most kids, the more you do imagination exercises, the less stress you'll feel—and the warmer your fingers and hands will get!

Biofeedback Card
Use only at room temperature
(70˚ to 74˚F, 21˚ to 23˚C).
Hold your thumb in the black box below for a count of ten, then compare the box color to the color key at bottom to see your stress level.

Be the
BOSS
of your
BODY

MOST STRESSED   STRESSED   SOME STRESS   RELAXED

Self-talk is how we talk to ourselves while we are doing things.

You can use positive (helpful) self-talk to help you manage difficult situations. Think of this as being a good coach to yourself. You can improve your thinking, increase your ability to relax, and be healthier by practicing positive self-talk.

When to Use It: Use You're the Coach regularly to keep your body, mind, and spirit healthy and balanced and to feel less worry or tension. You can also use You're the Coach whenever you start to feel stress building up, or when tension is causing headaches and stomachaches.

Why It Can Help: Scientific studies have shown that your thoughts affect how much stress you feel. Pleasant thoughts mean less stress!

What You Need: You need a positive attitude and a commitment to practice.

How to Do It: If you have a negative thought, replace it with a helpful one. It sounds simple, and it is—but you have to believe in the new thought, and you have to keep practicing. Hear your self-talk voice, and listen to it.

Here's a chart to help you think of some ideas. If you have a negative thought like the ones on the left side of the chart, you can replace it with the thought across from it on the right. Don't stop there, though. Think about all the negative thoughts you have and how you can turn each one into a helpful thought.

IF YOU THINK:	TRY THINKING:
I am really stressed out today.	I have a lot to do. I need to take care of myself.
Stress will ruin my day.	I will have a good day no matter what!
I know I won't sleep well tonight.	I will use my breathing and imagery to relax and sleep easily and comfortably.
I know I will fail the math test.	I have studied hard and will do my best on the test.
There's nothing I can do about stress.	I will listen to my body and take care of it in healthy ways. There ARE things I can do.

FUN FACT

About 300 thoughts a minute go through a person's brain.

Let Go and Get Loose is a fun way to get to know your body, learn to relax all of your muscles, and get rid of some of the stress you feel. You Let Go and Get Loose by tightening different muscle groups and then letting go, or releasing the tension until your entire body feels loose and relaxed.

When to Use It: Use Let Go and Get Loose whenever stress makes you feel uptight or aware of tight muscles.

Why It Can Help: The muscles in the back, shoulders, neck, head, and face can all be tight when you are stressed. When you tense up a muscle and then let it go, it actually relaxes more than it was before so you feel better.

What You Need: You need a comfortable place and a positive attitude.

How to Do It: Relax your muscles by tightening them for three seconds and then letting the tension go. After you tighten one group of muscles, move on to the next. Start with your toes and move up to your head. Here's how:

1. Tense the muscles in your feet. Hold to a count of three and let go.

2. Tighten your leg muscles from your toes to your hips. Hold to a count of three and let go.

3. Tighten your stomach area and your chest. Notice how hard it is to breathe. Hold to three and let go.

4. Pull your shoulders up to your ears. Hold to three and let go.

5. Tighten your arm muscles. Make fists with your hands. Hold to three and let go.

6. Clench your teeth and tighten your nose, cheeks, and eyes. Hold to three and let go.

7. Raise your eyebrows and tighten your forehead. Hold to three and let go.

8. Tighten your feet, legs, abdomen, chest, shoulders, arms, neck, and face. Hold and let go. Let every muscle in your body be completely loose and relaxed.

If you don't have a lot of time, you can also do this with just your shoulders, neck, face, and head. Remember to end with every muscle you tighten being relaxed.

B³

Have you ever walked into the kitchen after a bad day and noticed that you felt better once you smelled the comforting smells of dinner (or cookies!) in the oven? The change was real—you didn't imagine it! Good smells can actually help you feel better in many ways, including feeling more relaxed and comfortable. And that's what Aromatherapy is: using smells to help you feel better. In Aromatherapy, you use oils from plants like lavender, peppermint, and rosemary, and also from fruits like orange, lime, and lemon. These are called "essential oils."

When to Use It: Use Aromatherapy whenever you feel stressed. It's helpful to smell your favorite oil at the same time you are doing a relaxation exercise such as Belly Breathing or Imagine That! They work well together to get your body even more relaxed than either one can do alone.

Why It Can Help: The nerve from your nose has a connection to deep areas of your brain. That connection has a powerful effect on how your body feels.

Yum!

B³

What You Need: You need high-quality essential oils, which you can buy at health food stores, at natural food co-ops, at some drugstores, and on the Internet. Ask for medical type oils so you know they are of good quality. Look for oils that say "organic" on them—that means they should be all natural.

Here's a list of what different oils can help with:

+ For relaxation and better sleep, use sweet orange, lavender, and sandalwood.

+ For pain, use rosemary, chamomile, and peppermint.

+ For upset stomach, use ginger and spearmint.

Important:
To be safe, get a parent or another adult to help you buy aromatherapy oils and do this activity.

Essential oils

42

How to Do It: Unscrew the cap from the bottle, hold it about one inch from your nostrils, and inhale slowly and deeply. Repeat once or twice. Each time you inhale, imagine the healing scent traveling into your brain and sending out healing messages to your body. To enjoy oils any time, all day long, place one or two drops of oil on a tissue or cotton ball and carry it with you. Then you can smell it several times a day.

If you spill essential oil, be sure to wear gloves when you wipe it up, because the oil could irritate your skin. If you get some oil on your skin, put a little vegetable oil on it and wipe it off (gently). If you accidentally splash oil in your eyes, flush your eyes with milk (whole milk if you can) and then rinse them with water. Get medical attention right away.

Chamomile

Sniff...sniff

Skill 6: Acupressure

Acupressure was developed in East Asia (countries like China and Japan) about 5,000 years ago. It means applying pressure to specific spots on your body that can help you feel better. For example, if you feel stressed, there is a very powerful point on your forearm (see diagram on page 47) that can make you feel better just by pushing on it. You have more than 300 of these spots, all over your body, for treating all kinds of symptoms, including stress.

Traditional Chinese culture describes a life force, or "Qi" (pronounced "chee"), that flows through each person on special pathways. When these pathways become blocked, **Acupressure** can unblock them so your Qi flows freely, making you feel more energized and healthy.

When to Use It: You can push on your acupressure points any time you want to feel more relaxed. You can also push on them throughout the day, even when you are not stressed, just to keep things in balance.

Why It Can Help: Each acupressure point is connected by your nervous system to a place in your brain that controls a particular symptom (like anxious feelings, tension, stomachaches, or not being able to sleep). Pressing on the right acupressure point helps the body release feel-good chemicals (endorphins) to relieve that symptom. Stimulating these points also reduces tension and stress, relaxes muscles, and allows better blood flow. That helps oxygen and nutrients move through your body, and strengthens your immune system, too!

What You Need: You can stimulate these special acupressure points using
+ your finger
   + a pencil eraser
      + an acupressure band or beads
         + a wooden acupressure tool

Acupressure tool

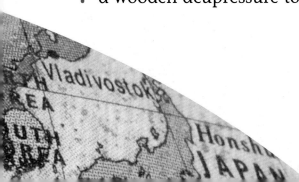

45

How to Do It: Look at the acupressure points diagrams on page 47 and select a point you want to stimulate. Good places to start are the Anxiety Points. One, called "Spirit Gate," is located on the inside of your forearm, on the wrist crease in line with your little finger. Another, called the "Third Eye Point," is located right between your eyebrows at the top of the bridge of your nose. Once you've selected a point, push on it using your finger, an acupressure tool, or another tool for 30 seconds to one minute. Use medium pressure, making small circles. Repeat this every 15 minutes and take a few Belly Breaths after each stimulation.

Keep Practicing

Once you have practiced all the B³ skills a few times, figure out which ones work best for you. Maybe you like using them all. If so, great! Whichever skills you use, remember to keep practicing them regularly, even when you are feeling fine, so you're comfortable with them and they become part of your everyday life. That way you'll be able to use them easily when you're feeling stressed. You'll also prevent some stress from forming in the first place.

Third Eye Point

Between your eyebrows, in the dip where the top of your nose and the bottom of your forehead meet, this point relaxes your nerves.

Inner Gate

Located in the middle of the inside of your wrist, two and one-half finger widths above your wrist crease, this point helps to release anxiety.

Spirit Gate

This point, found on the inside of your wrist crease, in line with your little finger, can help you settle down if you're very excited.

Crooked Marsh

On the inside of the arm where it bends, this point relaxes you and can help relieve stomachaches that come from stress.

Sea of Tranquility

On the center of your breastbone, this point helps to release anxiety and negative emotions.

47

Feel Good Every Day

Another important part of being the boss of your body is improving your lifestyle habits. "Lifestyle" means all the basic things you do every day, like sleeping, exercising, eating, doing activities, going to school, and enjoying hobbies. Since you do these things every day, it's easy to forget about how big a part of your life they are. If you make changes in your lifestyle you can do a lot to reduce stress and any aches and pains it may cause you to feel. Check out these ideas for getting healthier in several lifestyle areas. To begin with, choose two or three areas where you would like to improve, and try some of the ideas. Later, you can improve other areas. Even small changes can make a big difference!

Give Yourself a Break: Life Management

● Don't commit yourself to too many activities. Even if all the things you're doing are fun, you can really wear yourself out if you don't have enough downtime. ● You don't have to be perfect or be the best at everything you do. It's important to do as well as you can at things, but try to remember that nobody is perfect.

Eat Well and Feel Super: Your Diet

● Eat a broad variety of foods including lots of fruits and vegetables of different colors. A variety of foods means a variety of nutrients for your body. ● Eating smaller meals and snacks regularly throughout the day may be better than eating large amounts of food less often, because it helps your energy level stay even. ● Eat more **whole foods** and fewer **processed foods** (whole foods are fresh, natural foods that haven't been changed or prepared; foods that *have* been changed or prepared are processed). Whole foods provide more nutrients and none of the unhelpful extra stuff that comes in processed foods (like artificial dyes and sweeteners). ● Eat organic foods (natural foods that have been grown without the use of artificial chemicals) whenever possible. ● Drink plenty of water every day to keep your body working its best.

Move More, Feel Better: Exercise

● Do something active by yourself—like walking, biking, or swimming—for at least 15 minutes, five days a week!

● Play team sports such as soccer, baseball, lacrosse, volleyball, or basketball. ● Get flexible. Try yoga, dance, gymnastics, or tai chi.

49

Clues to a Healthy Snooze: Your Sleep

● Everybody is a little bit different, but most kids and teens need nine to 10 hours of quality sleep each night to restore and refresh their body, mind, and spirit.

● Bedtime routines are important because they help your body, mind, and spirit get ready for sleep. Make your routine similar every night: for example, brush your teeth, wash your face, and listen to relaxing music. Use B³ skills such as Belly Breathing, Imagine That! or Aromatherapy to help you relax and feel positive emotions when you go to sleep. ● Sleep in a dark room without any computer screens, televisions, or lamps on (a night light is okay). In the morning, make sure to get exposed to natural light as soon as possible. This will help set your body clock to your wake and sleep schedule.

Take Care of Your Inner Self: Spiritual Stuff

● Take pause. Spend 15 minutes each day on quiet reflection, prayer, or meditation. ● Keep a "Gratitude Journal." Every day, write down three things you are thankful for. Also, tell someone in your life why you appreciate him or her.

● Enjoy nature. Take a stroll in a park or, if you can, walk through woods, or by a lake or river. Enjoy gardens and flowers along city streets. ● Find and appreciate beauty. Go to art galleries or museums or listen to music. ● Create. Paint, draw, sculpt with clay, play music, or do crafts. ● Volunteer to help. Helping and supporting others feels great.

Connect with People: Social Supports

- Have a good laugh with family and friends every day—tell jokes, watch a silly movie or TV show, check out a funny Web site, or put on a goofy play together. • Do activities with family or friends. For example, play games, go to the zoo, go sightseeing, play with animals, rake leaves, or take walks. • Eat breakfast, lunch, or dinner with friends and/or family. Don't have the TV on or anything else that could distract you during the meal. Don't answer the phone, either. Instead, pay attention to each other. Take your time, relax, and talk. • Hang out with friends outside of school. Play and have fun. If you're too busy, call them up to say hello.

Keep Track of Your Progress

Being the boss of your body gives you a lot of power over your health, but you have to stick with it. It can be a slow process at first, but if you don't give up and you continue to practice, you'll get better at the B³ skills—and you'll feel better and better.

To help yourself stay excited and confident about being the boss of your body, even when it seems hard, keep track of your progress. This helps to show you that you are getting better, even if sometimes it doesn't feel like it. Remember your whole-self checkup on pages 18–27? Do those exercises every day and notice how your feelings change. It won't be long before you'll see some real improvement.

Stick with It!

You have a lot to be proud of: you have tons of natural talent to balance and heal yourself and live healthier. With a positive attitude and a commitment to practice, you have everything you need to

- be the boss of your stress
- be the boss of your body
- **and be the boss of your life!**

53

A Note to Grown-Ups

Many experts believe that children today are more stressed than ever before. Reasons for this may include living in a fast-paced world and increased pressure on younger and younger children. Many of today's kids have full schedules and expectations that rival those of adults. But unlike most adults, many children haven't learned positive ways to handle stress in their lives.

The self-care skills in this book are a powerful tool children can use on their own to take control of their health and wellness—and their stress. Studies show that kids who have practiced these skills and who feel confident about their role in their health and wellness handle stress much better than kids who don't. By encouraging the children you know to read this book and practice the skills in it, you are giving them a great gift they can use the rest of their lives.

About Self-Care Skills

As recently as 30 years ago, it was not widely accepted (in Western medicine) that people could control physical activities like their breathing, heart rate, blood pressure, skin temperature, or perspiration level. Now, we know not only that people can control these (all of which influence our experiences of stress), but also that the way people think about their health or illness has a lot to do with how they feel physically. We also know that skills like the ones in this book can have a huge ongoing impact on people's health.

Surgery, medicine, and other medical interventions all have their place and are sometimes necessary. However, much of the time self-care skills are a safer, less invasive, more natural—and self-directed—way for people to lead healthy lives. Kids and families can create and maintain an optimal level of health and wellness by using these skills and by making improvements to lifestyle aspects such as diet, sleep, and exercise.

Your Role as a Coach

The Be the Boss of Your Body (B[3]) series is about kids taking charge of their own health, but that doesn't mean kids don't need help from adults. Adults who help kids with the B[3] skills are called coaches. Any caring adult can be a coach to a child in pain—including a parent, grandparent, sibling, healthcare professional, school nurse, teacher, or friend. Being a coach means supporting the child in the process of learning these skills and making lifestyle changes. Kids need encouragement when the process seems hard or slow; they need positive reinforcement when they practice; and they need love and support when they are not feeling well.

What are the most important things you can do to provide this support?

- Read this book to gain a better understanding of what your child is doing.
- Be available and supportive when your child feels uncomfortable.
- Help children to identify their stressors.
- Set realistic expectations for behavior, academics, and activities.
- Give praise and positive reinforcement for using the skills; celebrate the child's successes and strengths.
- Encourage your child to continue participating in school and favorite activities.
- Engage in self-care skills yourself.

Evidence suggests that people who engage in self-care activities live healthier, more productive lives. Teaching kids to look at their health from a holistic perspective—considering body, mind, and spirit—and teaching them self-care skills sets the stage for lifelong wellness and balance. By encouraging and helping your children with the skills in this book, and modeling the skills yourself, you can give them the confidence to uncover the wealth of talent and strength they possess and encourage them to actively participate in their health. These skills can make a positive difference in *your* life, too!

Please remember that this book is not intended as a replacement for professional medical or psychological consultation when this is needed. Children and adolescents who are having serious health problems or new onset of symptoms should be evaluated by their primary care provider. Stress that causes children to experience severe changes in mood, sleep or dietary disturbances, or serious physical symptoms (such as fever and vomiting) needs to be evaluated and treated by a qualified healthcare professional.

Glossary

acupressure: applying pressure to specific spots on your body to help you feel better. Go to pages 44–47 to learn how to do it.

aromatherapy: using healing smells from natural plant oils to help you feel better. Go to pages 40–43 to learn more.

balance: you are balanced when your mind, body, and spirit are healthy and positive, adding up to a whole, healthy, fabulous you! Check out pages 8–9 to learn more about what this feels like.

endorphins: natural chemicals your body releases to reduce pain. You can learn ways to get your body to release endorphins on pages 30 and 45.

essential oils: oils that give plants their smells and that are used in aromatherapy. To read more, go to pages 40–43.

self-care: things you can do yourself to take care of yourself. That's what this book is about!

spirit: the part of you, deep inside, that gives you feelings of hope, comfort, and peace and gives life meaning. Go to page 7 to learn more.

About the Authors

Timothy Culbert, M.D., is a behavioral and developmental pediatrician with training in biofeedback, medical hypnosis, and holistic medicine. He is the medical director for the Integrative Medicine Program at Children's Hospitals and Clinics of Minnesota. Tim gives presentations nationally and internationally and publishes widely on mind-body skills training with children and teens. He has helped kids in clinical practice for 15 years, with special interests in teaching kids self-care skills.

Tim lives in Greenwood, Minnesota, with his wife, Heidi, and teenage children, Sam and Hannah. He enjoys traveling, cooking, writing, hiking, and various creative endeavors.

Rebecca Kajander, C.P.N.P., M.P.H., is a nurse practitioner at the Alexander Center, Park Nicollet Health Services of Minnesota. She has treated children and adolescents for nearly 40 years, has helped hundreds of children take care of themselves using self-care skills, and helped many more understand and live with ADHD. In 2000, Rebecca was named "Pediatric Nurse Practitioner of the Year" by the Minnesota chapter of the National Association of Pediatric Nurse Practitioners.

Rebecca has been a lifelong resident of Minnetonka, Minnesota. She's married and has a grown son. When not working, Rebecca enjoys yoga and doing just about anything outdoors.

Fast, Friendly, and Easy to Use
www.freespirit.com

Browse the catalog **Info & extras** **Reliable resources** **Many ways to search** **Quick check-out** **Stop in and see!**

Our Web site makes it easy to find the positive, reliable resources you need to empower teens and kids of all ages.

The Catalog.
Start browsing with just one click.

Beyond the Home Page.
Information and extras such as links and downloads.

The Search Box.
Find anything superfast.

Your Voice.
See testimonials from customers like you.

Request the Catalog.
Browse our catalog on paper, too!

The Nitty-Gritty.
Toll-free numbers, online ordering information, and more.

The 411.
News, reviews, awards, and special events.

 Our Web site is a secure commerce site. All of the personal information you enter at our site—including your name, address, and credit card number—is secure. So you can order with confidence when you order online from Free Spirit!

For a fast and easy way to receive our practical tips, helpful information, and special offers, send your email address to upbeatnews@freespirit.com. View a sample letter and our privacy policy at www.freespirit.com.

1.800.735.7323 • fax 612.337.5050 • help4kids@freespirit.com